The Pre-Trib Rapture

The great escape or the

great deception?

Elwood Trost

STUDIO
OF BOOKS
THE SPACE FOR YOUR MESSAGE

Studio of Books LLC
5900 Balcones Drive Suite 100
Austin, Texas 78731
www.studioofbooks.org
Hotline: (254) 800-1183

Ordering Information:
Special discounts are available on quantity purchases by corporations, associations, and others. For details, contact the publisher at the address above.

Printed in the United States of America.

ISBN-13: Softcover   978-1-968491-91-8
          Ebook   978-1-968491-92-5

Table of Contents

"About the Time of the End, a body of men will be raised up who will turn their attention to the prophecies, and insist on their literal interpretation in the midst of much clamor and opposition."~ Sir Isaac Newton

Whose voice then shook the earth; but now He has promised, saying, "Yet once more I shake not only the earth, but also heaven. Now this, "Yet once more," indicates the removal of those things that are being shaken, as of things that are made, that the things which cannot be shaken may remain. Therefore, since we are receiving a kingdom which cannot be shaken, let us have grace, by which we may serve God acceptably with reverence and godly fear. For our God is a consuming fire (Hebrews 12:26-28).

My people are destroyed for lack of knowledge (Hosea 4-6a).

ENDORSEMENTS

"As the Lord's return draws near, He is raising up voices; calling upon His people to awaken out of our slumber because our salvation is now nearer than when we first believed. As John the Baptist did before the Lord's first coming, they are calling upon the people of God to repent. Also, preparing the way in their hearts, because once again the kingdom of God is close at hand. is one of these voices. It is high time that the Church should awaken and prepare herself as the espoused Bride of Christ. It is imperative that the Church recognizes the hour in which she finds herself and begins to sharpen her focus on end-time events –putting to the test commonly held beliefs. We can no longer afford ourselves the luxury of saying, 'It will all pan out in the end.' I am grateful to for being obedient to his call and making his voice heard as he does in this book."

-George Sidney Hurd
Missionary and Author; Mitu, Colombia

"The most powerful, paradigm changing books ever written have gone against the flow and dramatically redirected the current of prevailing beliefs. This book by is such a book. The Lord's armies currently in America have been lulled to sleep by resting in the belief that they will escape by 'rapture' the difficult days ahead. This book will wake them up, eradicate the flight response and initiate intercession for what is coming to planet Earth!"

-Bill Sawyer, *Founder and Former CEO of Networking in Christ.*

Which is it? Pre-Trib? Mid-Trib? Pre-Wrath? Post-Trib? The Pre-Tribulation Rapture: The Great Escape or The Great Deception? Gives a good explanation into all the rapture theories and excellent insight in what the Bible has to say about the last days. has done his homework!"

-Deb Feist, Author

(Listening Prayer; How to Hear the Voice of God; Pursuit of happiness; Musings: A Theology Book by a Nontheologian for Non-Theologians; Tears of Longing; Jesus of the Gospels)

FORWARD

by Greg Escher

Having grown up studying the Scofield Reference Bible, reading Hal Lindsey's The Late Great Planet Earth and listening to Larry Norman's song, "I Wish

We'd All Been Ready," I was a dyed in the wool Pre-Tribulation rapturist. When the Lord got a hold of my life as a young man, I began to devour the word. It was then that I discovered I John 2:27, "But the anointing which you have received from Him abides in you, and you do not need that anyone teach you..." I would let the Holy Spirit be my teacher. In my pursuit of becoming a teacher of the word, I availed myself of every tool I could lay hold of to give myself completely to an in-depth study of the Bible including the original languages and church history. Equipped with that knowledge, I began to realize that much of what was being taught in popular Christianity was simply a rehashed version of someone else's systematic theology. I began to rely very heavily on the words of Jesus that state, "If anyone wills to do His will, he shall know by concerning the doctrine, whether it is from God..." (John 7:17). That has been my hermeneutic: my approach to interpretation. He has been faithful to teach and guide me. He has answered every question I have ever had about doctrine. It was under the teaching ministry of Kingdom of the Cults author, the late Walter Martin, that I first was exposed to a scriptural challenge debunking . He used Revelation 20 to show that the first resurrection (i.e., the "rapture"), included the Great Tribulation saints. That was all I needed. A faithful search of all the texts revealed that each one presented the same scenario: the tribulation, Christ's coming and then the resurrection or the rapture. There no longer seemed to be any scriptural support for a secret, separate, and imminent rapture. It was then that I read, The Blessed Hope by George Eldon Ladd. He carefully chronicles the development and dissemination of the doctrine of and its beginnings just over a century ago. Unfortunately, almost every popular radio and television preacher teaches this doctrine. The effort made to defend it amazes me, yet I remain unconvinced and all the more determined to see this false doctrine exposed. I am thankful to my friend , who has been on a similar journey. He has done a great job with a simple explanation of the second coming. You will find his treatment very readable and packed with insights. Enjoy the journey...

-Greg Escher, pastor, Grace Community Church Fort Bragg, California

PREFACE

I have written this book to encourage God's children during these tumultuous times and how we can meet the coming days with love, faith, and hope.

We should not be divided over our view concerning when the rapture takes place, but it is important to know the truth about when it happens.

However, we do need to share our view in love and let the truth work itself out. We must keep the main thing the main thing which is for us to know the Lord and for the Lord to know us. Our salvation is based on that and not our view of when He returns. But at the same time, I think it is important to be seeking the truth about how the end-times unfold.

It is important to have a right attitude about The Great Tribulation and see it from a positive perspective as illustrated in the following story:

During the Vietnam War Admiral James Stockdale's plane was shot down over North Vietnam. He was taken prisoner and beaten very severely. He spent the next seven- and one-half years in captivity, and four years of that time was in solitary confinement. He was tortured many times. He made it through his ordeal mainly because of his attitude.

In a business book by James C. Collins titled, Good to Great, Collins writes about a conversation he had with Admiral Stockdale regarding his coping strategy during his captivity in a North Vietnamese Prisoner of War camp.

When Collins asked him about how he made it through such a difficult time. The Admiral answered:

"I never lost faith in the end of the story, I never doubted not only that I would get out, but also that I would prevail in the end, and turn the experience into the defining event of my life, which in retrospect, I would not trade."

Another thing that Admiral Stockdale accomplished was not only did he make it through, but he encouraged others and helped them through this time of trouble. Senator John McCain was one of them.

God is looking for men and women like Admiral Stockdale who have the right attitude to go through The Great Tribulation and to encourage others with the truth and to help them endure it.

In the book of Daniel, we read that there will be those that are here during The Great Tribulation sharing the truth to help others endure.

Those who do wickedly against the covenant he (the Antichrist) shall corrupt with flattery; but the people who know their God shall be strong and carry out great exploits. And those of the people who understand shall instruct many; yet for many days they shall fall by sword and flame, by captivity and plundering. Now when they fall, they shall be aided with a little help; but many shall join with them by intrigue. And some of those of understanding shall fall, to refine them, purify them, and make them white, until the time of the end, because it is still for the appointed time (Daniel 11:32-35).

The Great Tribulation will be a much greater event than the Exodus story. We will see the power of God released on the earth that will bring fear of the Lord back to the church with salvation, strength, and power.

Then I heard a loud voice saying in heaven, "Now salvation, and strength, and the kingdom of our God, and the power of His Christ have come, for the accuser of our brethren, who accused them before our God day and night, has been cast down. And they overcame him by the blood of the Lamb and by the word of their testimony, and they did not love their lives to the death. Therefore rejoice, O heavens, and you who dwell in them! Woe to the inhabitants of the earth and the sea! For the devil has come down to you, having great wrath, because he knows that he has a short time" (Revelation 12:10-12).

So hopefully, we also can say when it is all over as Admiral Stockdale said, "I never lost faith in the end of the story, I never doubted not only that I would get out, but also that I would prevail in the end, and turn the experience into the defining event of my life, which in retrospect, I would not trade."

The Great Tribulation will be "the worst of times and the best of times." It will be the worst of times because of the wickedness of man and how ungodly he has become. But it will also be of best of times because we will witness firsthand the revelation of Jesus Christ and His power, and the greatest revival of all time.

The end-time events of the second coming of Our Lord and Savior Jesus Christ are to remove the existing world governments and to replace them with the Kingdom of God. When Jesus returns, we will be caught up to meet the Lord in the air and escort Him back to earth to be part of His millennial reign. Heaven is coming to earth, not the other way around. The marriage supper of the Lamb will be on the earth with real food and real people, not in heaven.

God loves those who have accepted His Son Jesus, and He is dedicated to changing us into His image. He will give the earth to the meek, and they will help rebuild the ruined cities.

INTRODUCTION

The Bible is God's Holy Word and in it we may learn how to become children of God. It contains the meaning of life and gives us Divine Wisdom on how to successfully navigate through this life into a resurrected life. No wonder the Bible has sold more copies than any other book in history. The Holy Spirit is its author, and it is to be revered.

The Bible reveals to us how much God and Our Lord Jesus love us. When we believe in and accept Jesus and His sacrifice, God will never punish us because Jesus took our punishment upon Himself. Therefore, if we find ourselves here during The Great Tribulation, it is not because we are being punished, but it will be because we are being refined so we can rule and reign with Jesus.

The Bible is also history written in advance by the One who knows the future. If we study end-time prophecy and put it together piece by piece, we will get a clear picture of the end-times. We don't have to be Bible scholars to understand it. When we pray and ask God to lead us in our study of eschatology (the study of end-time events), He will answer our prayers and we will be able to comprehend it.

In his book The Vision by David Wilkerson, he describes the calamities coming to the earth that God has shown him. The book ends with this admonition to Christians:

"Prepared Christians-wake up! Everything is under control and God is at work. He is saving, healing, baptizing, and getting His house in order. To fear is blasphemy. We are commanded to encourage ourselves in the Lord and to begin to sing and rejoice as we see the final hour approach. Do I hear someone ask, 'But how can I rejoice when I see this old sin-cursed world fall apart?' My answer is the Bible answer: For we know that the whole creation groans and travails in pain…waiting for the redemption. (Romans 8:22-23). "A woman in labor may scream because of the pain, yet in her heart she rejoices because of the fact of new birth. The kingdom of God is coming. The kingdom of Satan is falling. So, the Christian can, with confidence, say: 'God has everything under control!'"

C. S. Lewis encouraged "resistance thinking, against popular trends that seek to make the gospel fit with the spirit of the age. We must speak the difficult and 'offensive' themes of the gospel as well as the more popular ones. The church's effectiveness lies in her calling to be against the world, yet for it."

Apostle Peter gives us some insight of the purpose for us being here during The Great Tribulation:

Blessed be the God and Father of our Lord Jesus Christ, who according to His abundant mercy has begotten us again to a living hope through the resurrection of Jesus Christ from the dead, to an inheritance incorruptible and undefiled and that does not fade away, reserved in heaven for you, who are kept by the power of God through faith for salvation ready to be revealed in the Last time. In this you greatly rejoice, though now for a little while, if need be, you have been grieved by various trials, that the genuineness of your faith, being much more precious than gold that perishes, though it is tested by fire, may be found to praise, honor, and glory at the revelation of Jesus Christ, whom having not seen you love. Though now you do not see Him, yet believing, you rejoice with joy inexpressible and full of glory, receiving the end of your faith— the salvation of your souls (I Peter 1:3-9).

The Apostle Peter tells us that our hope is in the resurrection not a Pre-Trib rapture and that our trials are to test our faith and our faith will come forth as gold. So, these end-time judgments are about our salvation and not our punishment. Just like the Israelites were set free from slavery by great tribulation from Egypt, we are going to be set free from the bondage of this world by the Great Tribulation.

Having an eternal mindset and what God is doing is the key to getting the victory, and we will need the power of the Holy Spirit operating in our lives to make it through these difficult days.

The Lord has shown me that the sword is coming, and it is my responsibility to get His Word out to those who will listen, and that they will start preparing for the shaking that is coming. The trials we are going through now are to deepen our relationship with the Lord so we will be able to stand in that "evil day." The apostles went about....

Strengthening the souls of the disciples, exhorting them to continue in the faith, and saying, "We must through many tribulations enter the kingdom of God" (Acts 14:22).

Sir Isaac Newton wrote, "It is our duty to search with all diligence into these prophecies. And if God was so angry with the Jews for not searching more diligently into the prophecies which He had given them to know Jesus the Messiah by, why should we think He will excuse us for not searching into the (End-Time) prophecies which He has given us to know the Antichrist by?.. The Antichrist was to seduce the whole world and therefore, he may easily seduce you if you are not well prepared to discern him. But if he should not be yet come into the world, yet amidst so many religions, of which there can (only) be but one true, and perhaps none of those religions that you are acquainted with, it is great odds, but you may be deceived and therefore it concerns you to be very circumspect" (cautious, watchful). ~ Sir Isaac Newton

So, let us be searching out these end-time prophecies? God has given us about 150 chapters in the Bible on the end-times because He knew that it was important for us to know them and how He is closing out this age.

Father, help us see through the deception of the enemy and help us be prepared for what we are about to experience. In Jesus' Name. Amen!

CHAPTER ONE

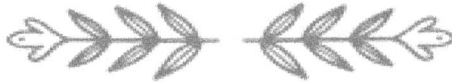

Daniel's 70th Week

There is a seven-year period that closes out this age referred to as Daniel's 70th week. These seven years are divided into two periods of three- and one-half years each. The first three- and one-half years Jesus referred to as the "beginning of sorrows," and the last three- and one-half years as The Great Tribulation:

For then there will be great tribulation, such as has not been since the beginning of the world until this time, no, nor ever shall be (Matthew 24:21). Daniel recorded it this way:

At that time Michael shall s tand up, the great prince who stands watch over the sons of your people; And there shall be a time of trouble, such as never was since there was a nation, even to that time. And at that time your people shall be delivered, everyone who is found written in the book. And many of those who sleep in the dust of the earth shall awake, some to everlasting life, Some to shame and everlasting contempt (Daniel 12:1-2).

Daniel is describing the resurrection which is our hope for the believers in Yeshua (Jesus). But just before the Resurrection there will be a time of unprecedented trouble. Our hope is not in escaping The

Great Tribulation, but in getting through it without losing our faith and receiving everlasting life. The Great Tribulation Is also God's harvest time when many will be saved. Therefore, many believers will be needed to bring it in.

The prophecy that reveals these last seven years is found in the book of Daniel 9:24-27:

Seventy weeks (seventy weeks of years or 490 years) are determined for your people and for your holy city, to finish the transgression, to make an end of sins, to make reconciliation for iniquity, to bring in everlasting righteousness, to seal up vision and prophecy, and to anoint the Most Holy (Daniel 9:24).

Daniel 9:24 is not fulfilled yet and as we go through the next couple of verses, we will see that sixty-nine weeks of years or 483 years of the 490 years have been fulfilled leaving one week of seven years to be fulfilled:

Know therefore and understand, that from the going forth of the command to restore and build Jerusalem until Messiah the Prince, there shall be seven weeks (49 years) and sixty-two weeks (434 years); the street shall be built again, and the wall, even in troublesome times (Daniel 9:25). And after the sixty-two weeks Messiah shall be cut off, but not for Himself; and the people of the prince who is to come shall destroy the city and the sanctuary. The end of it shall be with a flood, and till the end of the war desolations are determined (Daniel 9:26).

Jesus was crucified in or about AD 32. The temple was destroyed forty years later in AD 70 by a Roman army led by Titus, a Roman General. They tore down the temple stone by stone just like Jesus prophesied to get the gold out that ran down between them when the temple was burned.

Verses in Daniel 9:25 and 9:26 have been fulfilled leaving Daniel 9:27 to be fulfilled in our day.

Then he shall confirm a covenant with many for one week (seven years); but in the middle of the week, he (the Antichrist) shall bring an end to sacrifice and offerings; and on the wing of abominations shall be one who makes desolate, even until the consummation, which is determined, is poured out on the desolate" (Daniel 9:27).

These last seven years begin with a covenant being confirmed with many. Then, the Antichrist breaks the covenant and invades Israel halfway through these last seven years and the "abomination of desolation" is set up. The Antichrist then sits in the temple claiming to be God and whoever will not worship him will cast into prison or put to death. This is when The Great Tribulation begins. Jesus warns the people in Judea to flee into the mountains when they see the "abomination of desolation."

Another Scripture in Daniel referring to the Antichrist is:

He shall speak pompous words against the Most High, he shall persecute the saints of the Most High, and shall intend to change times and law. Then the saints shall be given into his hand for a time and times and half a time (3 ½ years) (Daniel 7:25).

But while the saints are given over to the Antichrist, the saints will receive power to defeat Antichrist at the same time. This appears to be an oxymoron, but if we look at the life of Jesus, we see that Satan had Jesus crucified but that Jesus defeated Satan by going to the cross. The saints overcome the Antichrist in the same manner by laying their lives down. This means salvation, strength, and power will return to the followers of Jesus Christ during The Great Tribulation.

Another Scripture in Isaiah that refers to the Antichrist and is the result of his short reign:

Those who see you will gaze at you, and consider you, saying: "Is this the man who made the earth tremble, who shook kingdoms, who made the world as a wilderness and destroyed its cities, who did not open the house of his prisoners?" (Isaiah 14:16-17).

In conclusion, The False Prophet working with the Antichrist brings down fire from heaven and performs signs and wonders and they will deceive many. Everyone whose name is not written in the Lamb's Book of Life will be deceived, and they will worship the Antichrist. The Antichrist will be credited with making the earth tremble, making it a wilderness, and destroying its cities.

If you have not accepted Jesus as your Lord and Savior, this would be a good day to do so. The end of the days is upon us, and those who accept Jesus Christ as Lord and Savior will experience everlasting life. Those that don't will experience the wrath of God.

CHAPTER TWO

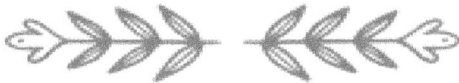

Types and Shadows

Types or shadows are history that have a prophetic message for our future. There are many of them in the Scripture that help interpret the end-time prophecies. I will share a few of them that I see.

This first Antichrist type I will share is from history and is not from the Bible but is a good example, Antiochus Epiphanies, who profaned the temple of God in Jerusalem by sacrificing a pig on the altar. He persecuted the Jews from 168 B.C. to 165 B.C. He was a Greek Hellenistic king who ruled the Seleucid Empire from 175 BC until his death in 164 BC.

Because Antiochus came from Assyria (now the Middle East) indicates that the Antichrist could be a Muslim from there. The ten nations the Antichrist will control are Muslim nations that surround Israel today and want to see her destruction.

President Erdogan of Turkey is currently restoring the Muslim Caliphate, which was dissolved in 1923. These are the same nations that used to make up Assyria. Erdogan is on the side of Hamas today and hates Israel. I am not saying he is the Antichrist, but he could be preparing a way for him. This could indicate that there is a good chance that the Antichrist comes from Turkey instead of Europe or the United States.

Now for a type and shadow I see from Scripture. One day when I was in prayer asking God how to put the judgments of Revelation together. This is what I heard, "Look at my instructions to Joshua for the battle of Jericho found in Joshua chapter six.

As I did, I saw that the battle of Jericho was a type and shadow of how the seals, trumpets, and bowl judgments of Revelation fit together and unfold chronologically.

The battle of Jericho lasted seven days and Daniel's 70th Week lasts for seven years, so if one day would equal a year, we can get an outline of the judgments of Revelation.

They marched around Jericho once a day for six days. This would represent the first six seals being opened in the first six years.

On the seventh day they were to march around Jericho seven times blowing their trumpets. This represents the seventh seal being opened the last year of the seven years with the sounding of the Trumpet Judgments. When the last trumpet sounded, they were to shout. This is a type of the second coming of Jesus at the "last trump."

The walls of Jericho falling symbolizing the destruction of the Antichrist, and Rahab and her family are brought out type of the resurrection/rapture.

Then, the army marched up and burned Jericho which is a type of Jesus' mighty army destroying the Antichrist in a military campaign recorded in Psalm 149: 6-9; Isaiah 63:1-6; Habakkuk 3:1-16).

This revelation places the wrath of God beginning the last year of Daniel's 70th Week which Jesus and His army completes after He returns and during the bowl judgments.

This also fits the pattern of birth pangs getting closer together and more intense. Seals would last seven years, the trumpets for twelve months, and the bowls for only days.

This also is some more confirmation for a Post-Trib rapture with Jesus coming at the "last trump." There is only days that separate Jesus' Second coming and Armageddon. I will explain more about this in my chapter on the feasts of the Lord.

God is our refuge and strength, a very present help in trouble. Therefore, we will not fear, even though the earth be removed, and though the mountains be carried into the midst of the sea; Though its waters roar and be troubled, Though the mountains shake with its swelling. There is a river whose streams shall make glad the city of God, The holy place of the tabernacle of the Most High. God is in the midst of her, she shall not be moved; God shall help her, just at the break of dawn. The nations raged, the kingdoms were moved; He uttered His voice, the earth melted. The Lord of hosts is with us; The God of Jacob is our refuge. Come, behold the works of the Lord, Who has made desolations in the earth. He makes wars cease to the end of the earth; He breaks the bow and cuts the spear in two; He burns the chariot in the fire. Be still and know that I am God; I will be exalted among the nations, I will be exalted in the earth! The Lord of hosts is with us; The God of Jacob is our refuge. Selah (Psalm 46:1-11).

In conclusion, there are many more types and shadows about the second coming of Christ, but these are all I will share for now. We are in a time of shaking before Jesus returns, and most of us need a closer relationship with Jesus by spending more time with Him in prayer and fasting.

Father, help us to get ready and give us the grace to reach many with the truth so they can be saved and delivered from experiencing Your wrath. In Jesus' Name. Amen!

CHAPTER THREE

God's Judgment or His wrath

In the Bible we read about God's judgment and His wrath. God's judgments are redemptive and are designed to bring repentance and salvation while His wrath is for the destruction of those who cannot be saved.

We can see both God's judgment and His wrath in John the Baptist's declaration about Jesus:

I indeed baptize you with water unto repentance, but He who is coming after me is mightier than I, whose sandals I am not worthy to carry. He will baptize you with the Holy Spirit and fire (judgment). His winnowing fan is in His hand, and He will thoroughly clean out His threshing floor, and gather His wheat into the barn; but He will burn up the chaff with unquenchable fire (the wrath of God). (Matthew 3:11-12).

We saw in the last chapter how in the first six seal judgments of Revelation were redemptive, a fulfilment of Jesus cleaning out His threshing floor and gathering His wheat into the barn. Then, Jesus will burn up the chaff with unquenchable fire. However, the 144,000 are sealed to go through the trumpet judgments and minister the gospel while being protected. Therefore, most of The Great Tribulation is redemptive and many are saved during this time:

Now when the dragon saw that he had been cast to the earth, he persecuted the woman (the woman is all believers in Yeshua, both Israel and Gentiles that are grafted in) who gave birth to the male Child (144.000). But the woman was given two wings of a great eagle, that she might fly into the wilderness to her place, where she is nourished for a time and times and half a time, (3½ years) from the presence of the serpent. So, the serpent spewed water out of his mouth like a flood after the woman, that he might cause her to be carried away by the flood. But the earth helped the woman, and the earth opened its mouth and swallowed up the flood which the dragon had spewed out of his mouth. And the dragon was enraged with the woman, and he went to make war with the rest of her offspring, who keep the commandments of God and have the testimony of Jesus Christ (Revelation 12:13-17).

Notice, the church is being protected for 3½ years not 2½ years as the Pre-Wrath rapture of the church teaches. We see that The Great Tribulation is God's harvest time which this next Scripture confirms:

After these things I looked, and behold, a great multitude which no one could number, of all nations, tribes, peoples, and tongues, standing before the throne and before the Lamb, clothed with white robes, with palm branches in their hands, and crying out with a loud voice, saying, "Salvation belongs to our God who sits on the throne, and to the Lamb!" All the angels stood around the throne and the elders and the four living creatures and fell on their faces before the throne and worshiped God, saying: "Amen! Blessing and glory and wisdom, Thanksgiving and honor and power and might, Be to our God forever and ever. Amen." Then one of the elders answered, saying to me, "Who are these arrayed in white robes, and where did they come from?" And I said to him, "Sir, you know." So, he said to me, "These are the ones who come out of The Great Tribulation, and washed their robes and made them white in the blood of the Lamb. Therefore, they are before the throne of God, and serve Him day and night in His temple. And He who sits on the throne will dwell among them. They shall neither hunger anymore nor thirst anymore; the sun shall not strike them, nor any heat; for the Lamb who is in the midst of the throne will shepherd them and lead them to living fountains of waters. And God will wipe away every tear from their eyes" (Revelation 7:9-17).

Now, if I was the enemy of God and wanted to stop this great harvest of souls that come into God's kingdom during The Great Tribulation, what would I do? I would slip into the church a doctrine that would convince many that they would not be here during The Great Tribulation, so they would be sleeping through the harvest and miss it.

Father, we pray You would wake us up and send laborers into the harvest. In Jesus' Name. Amen!

CHAPTER FOUR

The Seals of Revelation

In the book of Revelation, chapter five we read about a scroll that is sealed with seven seals. No one is worthy to open them except the Lamb of God. The scroll is the title deed to the earth and Jesus Christ is the only one who is worthy to open it. The seals are opened chronologically which means they follow one another.

There are seven seal judgments, seven trumpet judgments, and seven bowls judgments each getting closer together and more intense, like birth-pangs. The seventh seal contains releases the seven trumpet judgments, and the seventh trumpet introduces and releases the seven bowl judgments.

Jesus returns at the "last Trump" therefore, the bowl judgments are poured out after the resurrection/rapture that happens at the end of Daniel's 70th Week.

In chapter six of Revelation the Lamb starts opening the seals which gives us a description of what we can expect to see. There will be signs that appear to be similar before these, but we are not to confuse them with these final ones.

The seals of Revelation are the same events as Jesus prophesies about His second coming in Matthew chapter 24, Mark 13, and Luke 21; both put together give more revelation.

1st Seal: Deception, the first year of Daniel's 70th Week:

Now I saw when the Lamb opened one of the seals; and I heard one of the four living creatures saying with a voice like thunder, "Come and see. And I looked, and behold, a white horse. He who sat on it had a bow; and a crown was given to him, and he went out conquering and to conquer (Revelation 6:1-2).

Jesus answered and said to them: "Take heed that no one deceives you. For many will come in My name, saying, 'I am the Christ,' and will deceive many" (Matthew 24:4-5).

Apostle Paul warned about deception that would take place in the last days:

Now the Spirit expressly says that in latter times some will depart from the faith, giving heed to deceiving spirits and doctrines of demons (1 Timothy 4:1).

And:

Preach the word! Be ready in season and out of season. Convince, rebuke, exhort, with all longsuffering and teaching. For the time will come when they will not endure sound doctrine, but according to their own desires, because they have itching ears, they will heap up for themselves teachers; and they will turn their ears away from the truth and be turned aside to fables (2 Timothy 4:2-4).

2nd Seal: War, the second year:

When He opened the second seal, I heard the second living creature saying, "Come and see." Another horse, fiery red, went out. And it was granted to the one who sat on it to take peace from the earth, and that people should kill one another; and there was given to him a great sword (Revelation 6:3-4).

And you will hear of wars and rumors of wars. See that you are not troubled; for all these things must come to pass, but the end is not yet. For nation will rise against nation, and kingdom against kingdom (Matthew 24:6-7).

The second seal symbolizes war and ethnic division. And a great sword could indicate nuclear weapons being involved.

3rd Seal: Famine, the third year:

When He opened the third seal, I heard the third living creature say, "Come and see." So, I looked, and behold, a black horse, and he who sat on it had a pair of scales in his hand. And I heard a voice in the midst of the four living creatures saying, "A quart of wheat for a denarius, and three quarts of barley for a denarius; and do not harm the oil and the wine" (Revelation 6:5-6).

And there will be famines, pestilences, and earthquakes in various places all these are the beginning of sorrows (Matthew 24:7-8).

Because of the famines, and pestilences, and calamities many are starting to fall away from the faith, but many are also turning to the Lord and the gospel is going out and people are being saved. The world will be experiencing famine, pestilences, and earthquakes when the third seal is opened.

4th Seal: Death and Hades, the fourth year:

When He opened the fourth seal, I heard the voice of the fourth living creature saying, "Come and see" So I looked, and behold, a pale green horse. And the name of him who sat on it was Death, and Hades followed with him. And power was given to them over a fourth of the earth, to kill with sword, with hunger, with death, and by the beasts of the earth (Revelation 6:7-8).

We are now beginning into the last three- and one half years of Daniel's 70th Week. The Antichrist is the rider on the pale green horse which indicates that he is a Muslim. He invades Israel and stops the sacrifices and offerings, sets up the "abomination of desolation." He then sits in the temple claiming to be God. He is given power over one fourth of the earth that the ten nations surrounding Israel.

Jesus said:

"Therefore, when you see the 'abomination of desolation,' spoken of by Daniel the prophet, standing in the holy place" (whoever reads, let him understand "then let those who are in Judea flee to the mountains. Let him who is on the housetop not go down to take anything out his house. And let him who is in the field not go back to get his clothes. But woe to those who are pregnant and to those who are nursing babies in those days! And pray that your flight may not be in winter or on the Sabbath. For then there will be great tribulation, such as has not been since the beginning of the world until this time, no, nor ever shall be. And unless those days were shortened, no flesh would be saved; but for the elect's sake those days will be shortened" (Matthew 24:15-22).

Jesus is warning them about the Antichrist attacking Israel. In Luke chapter 21:20, Jesus says when you see the armies surrounding Israel, that those that are in Judea are to flee into the mountains.

5th Seal: Martyrdom, the fifth year:

When He opened the fifth seal, I saw under the altar the souls of those who had been slain for the word of God and for the testimony which they held. And they cried with a loud voice, saying, "How long, O Lord, holy and true, until You judge and avenge our blood on those who dwell on the earth?" Then a white robe was given to each of them; and it was said to them that they should rest a little while longer, until both the number of their fellow servants and their brethren, who would be killed as they were, was completed (Revelation 6:9-11).

Then they will deliver you up to tribulation and kill you, and you will be hated by all nations for My name's sake. And then many will be offended, and will betray one another, and will hate one another. Then many false prophets will rise up and deceive many. And because lawlessness will abound, the love of many will grow cold. But he who endures to the end shall be saved. And this gospel of the kingdom will be preached in all the world as a witness to all the nations, and then the end will come (Matthew 24:9-14).

When the fifth seal is opened, some of those destined for martyrdom will be martyred. Some will be jailed and others will be protected from the Antichrist.

6th Seal: Cosmic Signs, the sixth year:

I looked when He opened the sixth seal, and behold, there was a great earthquake; and the sun became black as sackcloth of hair, and the moon became like blood. And the stars of heaven fell to the earth, as a fig tree drops its late figs when it is shaken by a mighty wind. Then the sky receded as a scroll when it is rolled up, and every mountain and island was moved out of its place. And the kings of the earth, the great men, the rich men, the commanders, the mighty men, every slave and every free man, hid themselves in the caves and in the rocks of the mountains and said to the mountains and rocks, "Fall on us and hide us from the face of Him who sits on the throne and from the wrath of the Lamb! For the great day or His wrath has come, and who is able to stand?" (Revelation 6:12-17).

Cosmic signs are displayed at the opening of the sixth seal with the warning that the wrath of God is about to begin with the trumpet judgments. The trumpet judgments begin when the seventh seal is opened, and 144,000 are sealed to go them.

After these things I saw four angels standing at the four corners of the earth, holding the four winds of the earth, that the wind should not blow on the earth, on the sea, or on any tree Then I saw another angel ascending from the east, having the seal of the living God. And he cried with a loud voice to the four angels to whom it was granted to harm the earth and the sea saying, "Do not harm the earth, the sea, or the trees till we have sealed the servants of our God on their foreheads." And I heard the number of those who were sealed. One hundred and forty-four thousand of all the tribes of the children of Israel were sealed (Revelation 7:1-4).

We will see a great revival and harvest of souls brought into His kingdom during this time!

Seventh Seal: the seventh year, the wrath of God begins with the trumpet judgments:

When He opened the seventh seal, there was silence in heaven for about half an hour. And I saw the seven angels who stand before God, and to them were given seven trumpets. Then another angel, having a golden censer, came and stood at the altar. He was given much incense, that he should offer it with the prayers of all the saints upon the golden altar which was before the throne. And the smoke of the incense, with the prayers of the saints, ascended before God from the angel's hand. Then the angel took the censer, filled it with fire from the altar, and threw it to the earth. And there were noises, thunderings, lightnings, and an earthquake. So, the seven angels who had the seven trumpets prepared themselves to sound (Revelation 8-1-6).

In summary, the seals are opened chronologically. The first three seals Jesus referred to as the "beginning of sorrows." The "abomination of desolation" is set up and The Great Tribulation is ushered in when the fourth seal is opened. When the fifth seal is opened the persecution of Jews and Christians worldwide begins. When the sixth seal is opened the cosmic signs announce that the wrath of God is about to begin with the sounding of the trumpet judgments. The 144,000 sealed to go them through the trumpet judgments. The rest of God's people are protected during this time in a place God has prepared for them in the wilderness. Then, the seventh seal is opened, and the trumpets begin to sound and at the seventh trumpet or "last trump," the Lord returns, He gathers His wheat into the barn, burns up the chaff in the bowl judgments.

CHAPTER FIVE

Reasons I believe in a Post -Trib Rapture

For those who don't know what the rapture is; it is when we are caught up in the air to meet our Lord and Savior Jesus Christ and usher Him back to earth to rule the nations.

There are different views of when the rapture occurs. Let's look at them:

The Pre-Trib rapture view believes it will take place before the tribulation and could happen at any time. This view of the rapture became popular through a book of fiction by Tim Lahaye and Jerry B. Jenkins tilted Left Behind. This book became popular and sold millions of copies and was made into a movie.

I show how the Scriptures do not support this view, and how this is a fulfillment of the deception that Jesus and Apostle Paul warned us would happen in the last days.

Some believe in a Mid-Trib rapture that takes place in the middle of Daniel's 70th Week.

And then another view is in a Pre-Wrath Trib rapture that happens two thirds the way through Daniel's 70th Week at the opening of the sixth seal. They believe we will see the persecution of the Antichrist but will raptured before the trumpets judgments.

The Post-Trib rapture view believes the rapture will happen at the end of the seven years when Jesus returns at the "last trump." I believe this view is the most accurate according to Scripture while the other views have Jesus returning twice, instead of once. Also, this is the view is what Jesus taught.

So, let's look at what Jesus taught. In verse 15 of Matthew chapter 24, Jesus mentions the 'abomination of desolation" that takes place at the mid-point of Daniel's 70th Week and warns those in Judea to flee to the mountains. This is when the Antichrist invades Israel and stops the sacrifices and sits in the temple claiming to be God. This begins The Great Tribulation that will last for 3½ years until Jesus returns.

Then a few verses later in verse 21, Jesus refers to The Great Tribulation:

For then there will be great tribulation, such as has not been since the beginning of the world until this time, no, nor ever shall be (Matthew 24:21).

Then Jesus says He will return after that in verse 29 after the Great Tribulation:

"Immediately after the tribulation of those days the sun will be darkened, and the moon will not give its light; the stars will fall from heaven, and the powers of the heavens will be shaken. Then the sign of the Son of Man will appear in heaven, and then all the tribes of the earth will mourn, and they will see the Son of Man coming on the clouds of heaven with power and great glory. And He will send His angels with a great sound of a trumpet, and they will gather together His elect from the four winds, from one end of heaven to the other" (Matthew 24:29-31).

It could not be any clearer than Jesus tells us how and when the rapture will happen. So those believing in a Pre-Trib rapture make what Jesus taught void by saying Matthew chapter 24 pertains only for the Jews and not the Christians. This is interesting because I guess we can pick and choose what is for us in the New Testament.

Apostle Paul confirmed what Jesus taught in his letter to the Thessalonians:

Now, brethren, concerning the coming of our Lord Jesus Christ and our gathering together to Him, we ask you, not to be soon shaken in mind or troubled, either by spirit or by word or by letter, as if from us, as though the day of Christ had come. Let no one deceive you by any means; for that Day will not come unless the falling away comes first, and the man of sin is revealed, the son of perdition, who opposes and exalts himself above all that is called God or that is worshiped, so that he sits as God in the temple of God, showing himself that he is God (2 Thessalonians 2:1-4).

If we want the truth, we will have to admit that these verses I just shared debunk a Pre-Trib rapture if we don't make Scripture say something that it does not say.

It is important to know the truth because the truth will help us endure to the end and our salvation depends on that.

Jesus said:

"But he who endures to the end shall be saved" (Matthew 24:13).

CHAPTER SIX

The Feasts of the Lord

Spring Feasts: Fulfilled at the first coming of Jesus

Feast of Passover	Nissan14	Leviticus 23: 4-5	Fulfilled by Christ the Lamb of God on the Cross
Feast of Unleavened Bread	Nissan15	Leviticus 23:6-8	Fulfilled by Christ by living a sinless life
Feast of First Fruits	First day after the Sabbath	Leviticus 23:9-14	Fulfilled by Christ by His resurrection

Fifty days after Feast of First Fruits

Feast of Weeks or Pentecost	Fifty days after Feast of First Fruits	Leviticus 23:15-22	Fulfilled on the Day of Pentecost

Fall Feasts: Six months after Spring Feasts to be fulfilled at the second coming

Feast of Trumpets	Tishri 1	Leviticus 23:23-25	Jesus Returns at the "Last Trump"
Day of Atonement	Tishri 10	Leviticus 23:26-3	Armageddon
Feast of Tabernacles, Feast of Ingathering	Tishri 15	Leviticus 23:33-35	Marriage Supper of the Lamb

The seven feasts of the Lord are prophetic and reveal how the first and second coming of Jesus unfold. Jesus fulfilled the spring feasts exactly to the day and hour. He was crucified on Passover, put in the grave on Unleavened Bread, and resurrected on the feast of First fruits.

Fifty days later Pentecost was fulfilled when the Holy Spirit baptized the 120 in the Upper Room. The First four feasts have been fulfilled leaving the three fall feasts to be fulfilled at the second coming of Jesus. The summer between the spring feasts and the fall feasts is representative of the last 2,000 years.

It is interesting that the Feast of Trumpets is the only feast out of the seven that begins a month which is the month of Tishri. All the other six feasts fall in the middle of the month on a full moon. For the Feast of Trumpets to begin two rabbis need to witness the sliver of the new moon. However, clouds could obscure the moon and witnesses are required. The rabbis later added a second day to this feast to make sure they didn't miss it. Was Jesus giving us a clue that He would be returning on the Feast of Trumpets because no one knew the day or hour. Apostle Paul told us we would know the season of the return of the Lord:

But concerning the times and the seasons, brethren, you have no need that I should write to you. For you yourselves know perfectly that the day of the Lord so comes as a thief in the night. For when they say, "Peace and safety!" then sudden destruction comes upon them, as labor pains upon a pregnant woman. And they shall not escape. But you, brethren, are not in darkness, so that this Day should overtake you as a thief. You are all sons of light and sons of the day. We are not of the night nor of darkness. Therefore, let us not sleep, as others do, but let us watch and be sober. For those who sleep, sleep at night, and those who get drunk are drunk at night. But let us who are of the day be sober, putting on the breastplate of faith and love, and as a helmet the hope of salvation 1 Thessalonians 5:1-8).

We are to meet what is coming with love, faith, and hope.

One advantage if the Post-Trib rapture is true, we can know the Feast of Trumpets that Jesus returns even if we cannot know the day or hour. This is because when we see the Antichrist is sitting in the temple claiming to be God which Jesus referred at the "abomination of desolation." Then, we can expect Jesus to return 3½ years Later on the Feast of Trumpets.

Let's look now at how the fall feasts unfold. They begin with the Feast of Trumpets on Tishri one. Ten days later, the Day of Atonement begins on Tishri ten. Five days after that the Feast of Tabernacles begins on Tishri 15.

So, the Lord returns on the Feast of Trumpets and the resurrection/rapture happens. The resurrected saints become His mighty army (Psalm 149:6-9; Joel 2:1-11). Then, Jesus leads a military campaign up and into the promised land of Israel. (Deuteronomy 33:1-3; Isaiah 63:1-6; Habakkuk 3:1-16).

This military campaign from the Feast of Trumpets to the Day of Atonement which is ten days. at which time Jesus reaches the Mount of Olives and Armageddon takes place. The kings of the East realize Jesus is marching towards Jerusalem and they surround the city to meet Him and are destroyed.

Five days later, on Tishri 15, the Feast of Tabernacles begin the "Marriage Supper of the Lamb." This is when Jesus will drink the fruit of the vine with us again on Mount Zion. The Marriage Supper of the Lamb happens here on earth with real food and wine.

I have shown you how we can piece together the puzzle of the last seven years of the Apocalypse according to Scripture and using a few types and shadows.

It is my prayer that your love, faith, and hope undergird you as you go through the testing of your faith during these difficult times, and you will endure to the end.

CHAPTER SEVEN

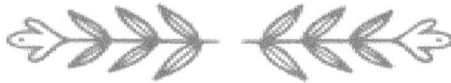

How We Can Prepare

What are some the of things that will help us get through the coming time of trouble.

1. Knowing the Truth

Jesus said, "And you shall know the truth, and the truth shall make you free" (John 8:32).

We are living in an age of deception and knowing the truth about why and what we are going to experience is important. Unfortunately, the people of God are not exempt from deception. We have an enemy that hates us and has infiltrated the church with a false hope that we will be raptured before The Great Tribulation. There is Scripture about us being protected during The Great Tribulation, but not escaping it.

In a letter written by Corrie Ten Boom, author and concentration camp survivor said, "She was talking to a bishop from a church in China," and he told her, "We failed our people by telling them there was going to be a Pre-Tribulation rapture and when the Communists took over in 1949, they persecuted and martyred millions of Christians." Many fell away because they were not prepared for this persecution. Corrie believed that persecution would come to the Christians of the West, and her advice was to read the Word, memorize Scripture, and encourage one another.

Meditating on the Word of God renews our minds and helps us see things the way God sees them.

It is only the Western church that believes in the false hope of a Pre-Trib rapture. The Christians in China, the Middle East, and Africa that are being persecuted today, don't believe in it.

We are to meet The Great Tribulation with faith and not to be in fear and knowing the truth that The Great Tribulation is our deliverance from this corrupt world.

2. Having a right Attitude:

"Therefore, do not worry about tomorrow, for tomorrow will worry about its own things. Sufficient for the day is its own trouble" (Matthew 6:34).

We are not to worry about what is coming, but we are to be watchful and aware and start preparing.

A prudent man foresees evil and hides himself, But the simple pass on and are punished (Proverbs 22:3).

It will be important to learn how to encourage ourselves in the Lord. There is story in the Bible about king David's army wanting to stone him because when they were gone to battle, the Amalekites raided his city and took their families captive and burned their city:

Now David was greatly distressed, for the people spoke of stoning him, because the soul of all the people was grieved, every man for his sons and his daughters. But David strengthened himself in the Lord his God (1 Samuel 30:6).

God answered David and gave him a strategy of what to do, and he was able to recover what was lost.

These days we are experiencing are distressing and they will be until our Lord Jesus returns. So, we need to learn to strengthen ourselves in Our Lord to get His strategies to help us stand against the enemy of our soul.

3. Deeping Our Prayer Life

Then you will call upon Me and go and pray to Me, and I will listen to you. And you will seek Me and find Me, when you search for Me with all your heart (Jeremiah 29:12-13).

When things are going on smoothy we tend to forget to pray, but things begin to shake a little, then we receive the motivation to pray.

If we will get serious with God in prayer, we will get results. Set some time aside each day to pray. We should start off every day with a quiet time with the Lord to enter His presence.

Enter into His gates with thanksgiving, and into His courts with praise. Be thankful to Him and bless His name. For the Lord is good; His mercy is everlasting, and His truth endures to all generations (Psalm 100:4-5)

Daniel and King David took time out three times a day to pray, and we need to take time out during the day to stay in His presence. This will help us build a solid relationship with the Lord and to hear His voice to help us get through the tough times. I believe Satan's strategy is to keep us busy with the cares of this life, so we don't have time to pray.

Keep on Praying:

Sometimes our prayers, even though they are always heard, are not answered right away. This is why Jesus asked us to persevere in prayer.

God showed me this principle once years ago when I was teaching a bible study to inmates. When I would drive home, I would drive by a local bar that was wild. I would pray for God to change it to something else. This went on for some time and my prayer wasn't being answered. Then one day I noticed a construction crew working on the bar. It was converted to a gas station and convenience store.

Later, I was buying gas at this station. I paid with a check and on my check, it said, I was in the firewood business. The owner took me out back and gave me all the wood from the remodel of the bar. Therefore, I had the privilege to burn that wood in my wood stove piece by piece.

What I took away from this experience was God was hearing me all along, but the timing had to be right for Him to answer my prayer.

P.U.S.H. Pray **U**ntil **S**omething **H**appens.

Then He spoke a parable to them, that men always ought to pray and not lose heart (Luke 18:1).

If we want to see more power in our prayers, let us add some fasting, worship, praise, and thanksgiving to them.

Be anxious for nothing, but in everything by prayer and supplication, with thanksgiving, let your requests be made known to God; and the peace of God, which surpasses all understanding, will guard your hearts and minds through Christ Jesus (Philippians 4:6-7).

4. Building Relationships with Other Christians

We need the fellowship of others who think and believe as we do.

"...Not forsaking the assembling of ourselves together, as is the manner of some, but exhorting one another, and so much the more as you see the day approaching" (Hebrews 10:25).

"One will chase one thousand, two will chase ten thousand." This is the principle of synergy which means that two people have much more power than one alone. Two horses can pull four times more than one horse can. So, as we come together, we become a powerful force.

Where two or three are gathered in His name I am in your midst (Matthew 18:20).

I, therefore, the prisoner of the Lord, beseech you to walk worthy of the calling with which you were called, with all lowliness and gentleness, with long-suffering, bearing with one another in love, endeavouring to keep the unity of the Spirit in the bond of peace. There is one body and one Spirit, just as you were called in one hope of your calling; one Lord, one faith, one baptism one God and Father of all, who is above all, and through all, and in you all. (Ephesians 4:1-6).

If we prepare by taking these simple steps, we will be able to endure to the end. And let us put on the Armor of God as will.

Finally, my brethren, be strong in the Lord and in the power of His might. Put on the whole armor of God, that you may be able to stand against the wiles of the devil. For we do not wrestle against flesh and blood, but against principalities, against powers, against the rulers of the darkness of this age, against spiritual hosts of wickedness in the heavenly places. Therefore, take up the whole armor of God, that you may be able to withstand in the evil day, and having done all, to stand. Stand therefore, having girded your waist with truth, having put on the breastplate of righteousness, and having shod your feet with the preparation of the gospel of peace; above all, taking the shield of faith with which you will be able to quench all the fiery darts of the wicked one. And take the helmet of salvation, and the sword of the Spirit, which is the word of God; praying always with all prayer and supplication in the Spirit, being watchful to this end with all perseverance and supplication for all the saints, and for me, that utterance may be given to me, that I may open my mouth boldly to make known the mystery of the gospel, for which I am an ambassador in chains; that in it I may speak boldly, as I ought to speak (Ephesians 6:10-20).

Father, I pray You will give me and my loved ones the strength to make it through these tumultuous days, and that we can meet them with faith and not in fear. Also, that we can have the boldness to share the gospel to those who need to hear it. In Jesus' Name. Amen!

CONCLUSION

I wrote this book to warn of the soon-coming Great Tribulation and the soon appearance of the Antichrist.

If you have never studied the end-time prophecies, I encourage you to search the Scriptures to see if what you believe is true. It is very important to know what God is doing in these times and to be on the same page with Him! The Scriptures will give us the faith to meet the challenges we are facing.

None of the church fathers believed in a Pre-Trib rapture, it has a recent origin, beginning with the visions of a young girl, Margaret McDonald, in 1830. This theory was picked up by Edward Irving, and was later popularized by C. I. Scofield, editor of the Scofield Reference Bible and by the Dallas Theological Seminary. This view is supported by using Scripture out of context.

In the introduction to this book, I gave some insights about the return of the Lord. There is no Biblical evidence of a two stage return or a rapture before the end of Daniel's 70th week. The argument that we are not "appointed to wrath," so we are raptured doesn't not hold up under closer examination of Scripture. Let's look at it:

For God did not appoint us to wrath, but to obtain salvation through our Lord Jesus Christ (1 Thessalonians 5:9).

This Scripture doesn't say anything about a rapture, and they add on to it say something it doesn't say which is speculation. Speculations don't build our faith, but the truth does.

Earlier in the book I reveal how it is only the last year of the seven years of Daniel's 70th Week that is considered the wrath of God, and the first six years are God's judgments which are redemptive. And it is only those who receive the mark of the beast that will endure the wrath of God. And the mark of the beast is only given out the last 3½ years during The Great Tribulation. Jesus threads "the Winepress of the Wrath" Himself after He returns.

Another verse used out of context to support a Pre-Trib rapture is this one:

Because you have kept My command to persevere, I also will keep you from the hour of trial which shall come upon the whole world, to test those who dwell on the earth (Revelation 3:10).

Jesus promises to keep us from the hour of trial which is to come upon the whole world. Let's look at the word "keep" in the Greek and see if it says anything about a rapture.

keep G5083 tēréō ----keep (380x) G5083 (70x) [Mounce Greek Dictionary] gk G5498 | s G5083 tēreō 70x

to **keep watch upon, guard.**

It means keep, watch upon, guard which indicates we are here and not raptured. This is another good example of how Scripture can be used to say something it doesn't say to support the false doctrine of a Pre-Trib rapture.

If God raptures His people before The Great Tribulation, it would be the first time He has taken His people out of tribulation, because in the past God has given His people strength to endure persecution which many of the nations are already experiencing. And these are the nations that are experiencing revival today.

The heroes of the faith in the eleventh chapter of Hebrews understood that their suffering would cause them to obtain a better resurrection. Nobody likes to suffer, but if we know it has a purpose, it does help us get through it.

Paul understood suffering was necessary to make him ready for the resurrection. So, what are we to believe? Shall we believe the radio and television personalities who preach the Pre-Trib rapture, and the movies and fiction novels like "Left Behind?" Do we want our ears tickled, or do we want the truth?

In my chapter on the Feasts of the Lord we saw how they are a rehearsal of the second coming of Jesus and give us more revelation.

I pray that you will keep your eyes on Jesus to make it through what is coming. Now is the time to start your training for reigning. It is a race, and though at times it may seem like a marathon, be of good cheer, because "you can do all things through Christ who strengthens you" and remember what Habakkuk declared:

Though the fig tree may not blossom, nor fruit be on the vines; Though the labor of the olive may fail, and the fields yield no food; Though the flock may be cut off from the fold, and there be no herd in the stalls. Yet I will rejoice in the Lord, I will joy in the God of my salvation. The Lord God is my strength; He will make my feet like deer's feet, and He will make me walk on my high hills (Habakkuk 3:17-19).

The End

www.ingramcontent.com/pod-product-compliance
Lightning Source LLC
Chambersburg PA
CBHW052124030426

42335CB00025B/3100